LIVING
DEBT FREE

LIVING
DEBT FREE

MATT SCHOENFELD

PRINCIPLES
FOR
ABUNDANT
LIVING

BEACON HILL PRESS
OF KANSAS CITY

Copyright 2008
by Matt Schoenfeld and Beacon Hill Press of Kansas City

ISBN 978-0-8341-2388-5

Printed in the
United States of America

Cover Design: Arthur Cherry
Internal Design: Sharon Page

Library of Congress Cataloging-in-Publication Data

Schoenfeld, Matt, 1967-
    Living debt free : principles for abundant living / Matt Schoenfeld.
    p. cm.
    Includes bibliographical references (p.   ).
    ISBN 978-0-8341-2388-5 (pbk.)
    1. Finance, Personal—Religious aspects. 2. Debt. I. Title.
    HG179.S296 2008
    332.024'02—dc22

                                                    2008034924

10 9 8 7 6 5 4 3 2 1

CONTENTS

INTRODUCTION

I'm sure you've seen the car insurance commercials featuring cavemen. They advertise that their product is so easy to use that even a Cro-Magnon man could figure it out. It's a clever idea, and it made me think that the same approach could probably be used for warning people about going into debt. Can't you picture the caveman saying, "Debt bad, cash good. Now let's go kill a wooly mammoth." Everyone knows that buying stuff you can't afford is not good. To my knowledge, staying debt free is so simple that even cavemen could do it. So why are so many smart 21st-century Christians falling into the debt trap?

Do you remember *Private Benjamin*, the movie Goldie Hawn starred in? She played Judy Benjamin, a sheltered, young, high-society woman. After she rashly enlisted in the Army, she began to miss the good life she left behind and lamented, "It's not the money—it's the stuff!"

From my experience as a Christian financial coach for more than a decade, I see that the problem many people are facing is the Private Benjamin complex. Similar to the out-of-place private and her cushy, pre-Army lifestyle, we like stuff. Further, we're constantly manipulated by the media and really important people such as movie stars and pro athletes who are paid to convince us that our stuff is not good enough or new enough. We dutifully commit ourselves to having new stuff whether we have the money to pay for it or not. Naturally, our new stuff is immediately not good enough or new enough anymore. And the beat goes on.

I want to explore with you an approach to getting out of debt that combines spiritual power from the Holy Spirit with practical strategies that will make your debt-reduction plan unstoppable, keep you out of debt for good, and provide the cure for "materialitus." "Materialitus" is an inflammation or swelling of one's material needs—a very contagious disease that is a common affliction among Americans and many others around the globe.

Biblical Approval for iPods

There's nothing inherently wrong with material possessions, by the way. I'm not one who believes that the only way you can please the Lord is to live in abject poverty while serving Him—unless, of course, the Lord calls you to sell it all and live that way. I believe that stuff is not bad, and stuff is not the issue unless we find ourselves so trapped by it, or our lives so cluttered up by it, or we become so fixated on getting more of it that our focus is not on wholesale devotion to following the Rabbi from Nazareth. The Bible tells us that money and the stuff it buys—iPods, a new Lexus—are fine. Okay, iPods and Lexus vehicles are not mentioned in the Bible, but money and mammon are. And the word *mammon*, roughly translated, means "stuff." The point is that Scripture neither condemns nor condones stuff. It does, however, *warn* us about it repeatedly.

In fact, regarding things we want or need, I've found that buying higher-priced products is often better stewardship of the money God has placed in my care. Higher-quality products more often than not last longer and cost less in the long run. However, falling in love with the stuff—the big-screen TV, the money, and perhaps the power that comes with it—is the real culprit. (See Hebrews 13:5.)

My observation is that a lot of folks—and I'm not letting myself off the hook here—are not in the position to hear if God tells us to sell it all, because the noise of the world is so loud in our ears. *Excuse me—did you say something, Lord? I'm getting some static on my end, because the latest and greatest special-effects movie is on televi-*

sion right now, and the explosions are really loud!
Our market-driven, materialism-inducing, noisy
culture is overtaking us. Do you ever long for five
minutes of quiet?

The last few summers, we've taken a family
trip to a very small town in the foothills of the
Sangre de Cristos mountain range. Here are
found no major attractions, no amusement
parks, no concert halls, no sports arenas! It's
awe-inspiring, because it's so quiet, peaceful, and
gorgeous. All there is to do in that sleepy area is
listen to God's voice in the wind, hike, watch the
deer and hummingbirds and bobcats and glory
of God's creation, and drink in the soul-refresh-
ing beauty of thunderstorms rushing through a
breathtaking mountain valley. This is the kind of
place where one can reconnect to the Father and
even hear His voice. Praying while you gaze at
the Rocky Mountains certainly seems to have a
powerful effect on the ability to hear what He's
saying. Maybe He's not calling you to sell everything you own, but maybe He does want to point
you toward a better way for dealing with culture,
debt, and money management.

I think most people know intuitively that debt
is bad. What we may not consider is that debt
has the power to block our intimacy with God

and our trust in Him. When our hearts are blocked off and stolen from God, it's devastating to our spirits. That's why debt is an effective and popular ploy Satan uses to keep our hearts from connecting with our Father. However, the implication of going into debt instead of trusting God for our provision is much more ominous. The stakes are much higher, and the global impact of God's people being in debt is far greater than any purely economic or fiscal effect. Here's the real reason consumer debt is so bad for God's people: *Consumer debt has the potential to make the ministry-funding pipeline go dry.*

The Empty Pipeline

According to Christian research expert George Barna,[1] only two percent of Christians under the age of 40 give 10 percent of their income to the Lord. Since 1999, only 6 to 14 percent of all believers who claim to be born again tithe, according to Barna's research. Consumer debt has the power to cripple the Church. If we Christians must give all our future money to the "credit card trinity," Visa, Master Card, and American Express, rather than the Triune God, how are we to fund the Great Commission?

Perhaps even more critical is the issue of servanthood. What I'm witnessing in my financial coaching ministry is that people can't serve the Lord because of their heavy debt loads. They're forced to delay God's call to missions, to serving youth, or to becoming pastors.

If your money is tied up in paying down unsecured consumer debt, your time is swallowed up working overtime, and your stress level is high, it can block your ability to love and serve others and can keep you from partnering with God in the Great Commission. Debt is deceptive and destructive.

I'm going to introduce you to a different approach to debt, because I know you're smarter than a caveman! Let's look at some realistic, simple, and effective ways for you to get out of debt.

ONE

DEVELOPING A STRATEGY OF LIVING WITHOUT DEBT

Wouldn't it be great to be totally debt free? Can you even envision that happening to you in your lifetime, including your mortgage? How do you think that would feel? When I ask people that question, I usually get answers like "Joy." "Relief." "Free." Or—"Yeah, right!"

If you want to be debt free, it's imperative that you have the vision first to see yourself as debt free. You must believe you can do this; it can't be just a nebulous aspiration. You must believe that God wants to do this work in your life. Philippians 4:13 says, "I can do all things through Christ who strengthens me" (NKJV). God's Word says *all* things—and that includes getting your debt paid off. Does it seem overwhelming or too good to be true?

You can do this, and the Lord wants to help you do it. However, the hard truth you must hear is that it's better to face this now, right at the start. Don't count on a magic wand to bail you out.

Inventing a Cure for Debt

Thomas Edison, the great inventor, said, "Many people miss opportunity because it's dressed in overalls and looks like work." You actually have a great opportunity before you to grow in your faith, grow as a person, change your life for the better, and experience a new-found level of joy and peace in your life. That's the good news. The bad news—or at least that's how you may see it right now—is that, as Edison said, a great deal of work is going to be involved to reap the benefits of this opportunity. But the benefits, as you will see, are gargantuan.

Becoming debt free must become your arduous pursuit. I'm not going to sugarcoat it either. I could recite platitudes and Christian clichés about victory and overcoming, but after serving for numerous years as the navigator for many families traveling down the debt-reduction road, I will tell you honestly that this process usually takes a few years.

Unfortunately, there are no quick fixes when it comes to getting out of debt. But there *is* opportunity to make your financial future and your life unbelievably better through the hard work of implementing your personal debt-reduction plan.

The wide road of indebtedness leads to destruction, but the narrow road of financial peace in Christ leads to life and blessing. Being in serious debt-reduction mode is like winning a grind-it-out, 12-round heavyweight boxing match. It won't be easy. There will be work and toil and sweat and probably quite a few tears. You may be thinking: *Can we reconsider the magic wand thing?*

The Narrow Road Leads to Debt Reduction

Stick with me. I'm not trying to scare you off, but I do want you to be realistic. You need to hear encouraging truth shared in love if you're to win the debt-reduction battle. You don't need more hollow, media-hyped, quick-fix schemes. That's wide-road stuff. But the narrow road leads to debt reduction. The painless, easy, overnight debt-reduction plans you hear about on radio and television are rubbish.

If you're struggling with paying off your debt, you're in a life-and-death battle for your financial future and certainly for your current or future marriage and family. Embarking on this road to debt reduction could literally change the entire future of your family line. The battle with debt you're locked in right now may be far bigger than you imagine. It may sound overly dramatic, but God's Word says you're involved in a flesh-and-blood struggle against rulers and authorities and powers of this dark world—spiritual forces of evil beyond the realm we live in or experience life in.

Drawing the Battle Lines

Ephesians 6:13 puts it this way: "Put on the full armor of God, so that when the day of evil comes, you may be able to stand your ground." The battle you're waging against indebtedness is a battle against evil in the form of a financial and spiritual foe. But God's Word tells you in advance that you will be able to win this battle.

In the following passage is a description of a set of tools you need for waging your successful debt-reduction battle:

Stand firm then, with the belt of truth buckled around your waist, with the breastplate of righteousness in place, and with your feet fitted with the readiness that comes from the gospel of peace. In addition to all of this, take up the shield of faith, with which you can extinguish all the flaming arrows of the evil one *(Ephesians 6:14-16).*

It's important that you enter your debt-reduction battle fully prepared to fight. God wants you out of debt so He can use you in the fullness of His plan, and He wants to protect your heart with the breastplate of righteousness so that you won't be crushed spiritually and emotionally by your debt. He wants you to be fit for readiness so you can experience financial peace in Him. And once you're ready and armed and full of faith to shield you from the tough times that will come while you're in debt-reduction mode, you'll have the ability to overcome the fiery darts of the evil one that will be thrown at you.

Don't be surprised if just as you start your plan to get out of debt, the car will break down, or you kids will get sick. You may very well have a fight with your spouse over money. But remember: your battle is not against flesh and blood. Stand firm. Then you have one more thing to do to be fully prepared for the battle:

> Pray in the Spirit on all occasions with all kinds of prayers and requests. With this in mind, be alert and always keep on praying *(Ephesians 6:18)*.

If you want to get really serious about getting out of debt, and I think you do or you would not have picked up this book, I encourage you to begin praying for your emancipation. If you're too feeble at this point to have the faith to pray, that's okay. Gather some trusted fellow Christians who will pray for you. This is where the battle will be won.

Even though implementing a debt-reduction plan will involve hard work and persevering through a tough battle, making your final payment will provide you with feelings of great accomplishment and spiritual victory. Last year two of my friends paid off their consumer debt within a week of each other. Talk about joy! I wish you could have heard their voices when they called me to tell me the good news. I want you to experience this joy and freedom too. The Lord, too, wants you to know this freedom. So put on the full armor of God, take up the sword of the Lord, pray in the Spirit, and make your stand.

Time for a Change

Now that you're all fired up to conquer your financial foe, you must be realistic in realizing that you can't use the "same old, same old" approach. Becoming debt free will become your number-one goal. Set a realistic date for when you want to reach your goal. Write Philippians 4:13 on your heart and mind: "I can do all things through Christ who strengthens me" (NKJV). Make this your theme verse. Ask the Lord to take over your finances, and commit to really changing your financial ways. I know it can be scary to relinquish control of your finances to God, and you'll need motivation and endurance to win this war. This book can help with that motivation, and the Lord will give you the endurance.

Think for a moment what you can do with the money that you'll free up when debt is behind you. Let's say it's an extra $500 or $1,000 a month. That will make a significant difference in your life. Will you save more each month? Give more? Travel? Those are all good answers, but they're all in the future. What about today?

After working for many years helping families organize their finances to get out of debt, I contend that you can live some of those future dreams now. If both the goal and reward are too far off, your drive to meet the goal and capture the reward will wane. Set the habits of giving or saving or traveling right now, while you're still in debt-reduction mode, or you probably won't do them in the future either.

Have you ever heard someone say, "If I won a big sweepstakes, I'd set up a special scholarship fund for inner city youth"—or perhaps make a huge donation to the church or go on regular missions trips. I tend to think that folks who don't do something toward realizing those goals, even on a very small scale, probably won't do them if they win a sweepstakes. Despite good intentions, I fear the Lord is not very impressed with sweepstakes-induced largesse. I think He would prefer even a humble effort today.

Instead, I suggest that your life will be a lot more rewarding if you agree to tutor a kid from the inner city right now, give some money to your church now, and take a short-term mission trip now—as long as none of these cause you to go deeper into debt. Do something today, while you're in debt-reduction mode, and watch how the Lord uses it to turn your tough situation into a precious gift to the Kingdom. You'll be so fulfilled from your service that some of the anxiety of being in a debt-reduction battle will melt away. It will revolutionize your debt-reduction plan.

Let's take a closer look at your foe.

ARE CREDIT CARDS REALLY THE ENEMY?

Let's get this clear right from the get-go: Satan is not manifested in little plastic rectangles with 16 numbers. Despite what you may have heard from prominent financial experts, credit cards are not the devil. The devil may be in the details, but he's not in credit cards.

No doubt, credit cards can cause you a world of hurt when misused, but the card itself is not the problem. The credit card companies are not even the problem. If you have high credit card debt, *you* are the problem!

The issue here is self-control. We read in 1 Peter 5:8, "Be self-controlled and alert. Your enemy the devil prowls around like a roaring lion looking for someone to devour." You and I are instructed to use self-control. This is not something we should expect God to do for us. If carrying credit cards causes you to buy stuff you can't afford, then by all means, ask the Holy Spirit to help you be alert to the temptation, and then cut those cards up. Ask God to show you why you buy things you can't pay for now. What is the real source of the temptation? The plastic card is only the tool by which you can succumb, not the temptation itself.

Cash, Check, or MasterCard?

Many will try to convince you that you'll spend more money if you use a credit card over other payment methods, but my observation is that you'll spend more money than you should *if you have no self-control,* not because you have a credit card. Regardless of the method of payment you choose, it can be abused if you fail to employ self-control. You can put all your cash into envelopes—a money management method of which I'm not a big fan—and still cause yourself financial distress if you don't exercise self-control. It can happen faster than you can say, "Let's go to Applebee's." There are plenty of people with no credit cards who are hooked on payday loans, rent-it centers, or pawn shops. In fact, I've seen many people spend more than they can afford or in irresponsible ways *because* they're using cash. Cash in hand is often cash gone.

How about checks? Same deal. Remember when overdraft protection used to mean that if you were a tad short on funds in the checking account you had a savings account to cover any checks that were presented during your cash crunch? Those were the days. Now overdraft protection usually means a line of credit. So if you're low on funds and write checks all day long, you still wind up with debt, because you are ringing up all your overdrafts onto the line of credit. By the way, that line of credit charges an interest rate that's similar to that of a credit card. Of course, you can skip the line of credit or the overdraft protection and do it the old-fashioned way—— bounce checks and pay costly overdraft fees.

Pick your poison. It's the lack of self-control that blocks people from living within their means, and lack of self-control is what causes us to misuse our financial tools. You know how a light appears on the dashboard or an alarm starts dinging if you forget to put on your seatbelt or you're running low on gas? Some cars in the 1980s even talked to you: "Your door is ajar." If only there were similar audio warnings when we're on the verge of spending money we don't have: "Put your wallet away. You sooo don't have the money for that!" Now that would be really helpful!

The Voice of Wisdom

Remember from the last chapter about praying to win the debt-reduction battle? Well, I believe we can ask God to provide that needed warning. God's Word says that His sheep will know the Shepherd's voice, and it's the Shepherd's job to protect the sheep from peril. It's your job to recognize the Shepherd's voice and heed His warning of peril.

Credit cards are just another financial tool—like cash or checks. One can do good or bad with any of these tools, so it's up to the individual. Credit card use is a perfectly fine means of making financial transactions if and only if—and believe me, it's a *big* "if" for a lot of folks—you use the card under the following three conditions. No exceptions.

Pay credit card balances in full each and every month, without fail. Sometimes people say to me, "Well, we always pay them off at some point during the year, so we just carry the balance for short periods of time." Nope, that's not what I'm shooting for. If you don't pay the total balance every single month, don't use them. Pick another method of payment. I often recommend checks with carbon copies to make tracking your expenses a snap. Use a credit card only if you pay zero dollars in interest and finance charges each and every year. My mother-in-law had the same credit card for more than 40 years, and she never once paid a nickel of interest on it. My wife and I are on year 17 of never paying a penny of interest for the convenience of this payment system.

Use the card in conjunction with the spending plan system that you'll find at <www.abundantlivingministry.org>. If you maintain a money management system that allows you to track your spending on a monthly basis so that you live within your means, it's irrelevant as to whether you pay by check, cash, credit card, or rubles. The spending plan will keep you from spending more than you have.

Use only cards that require no annual fee. With all the options available, there's no reason to hold a card that charges a fee.

My wife and I rarely carry cash. We conduct all our financial transactions by electronic payment, debit card, check, or credit card. If we have cash, we tend to spend it, often on stuff we don't need. You may be the opposite—you may tend to overspend if you use a credit card. You determine which method of payment works best for you. As the Greek philosopher Socrates is credited with saying, "Know thyself." Employ the Holy Spirit fruit of self control (see Galatians 5:22), be alert for the enemy, and use the payment method that gives you the greatest chance at living within your means.

Good Debt/Bad Debt

Further, just as credit cards are not little red men with horns and pitchforks, neither is all debt inherently evil. It's important to assess what kind of debt makes economic sense and what kind of debt is bad debt—both economically and spiritually. There are times that it makes economic sense to borrow money so that you can meet financial goals and other life goals. Let's turn our attention to good debt and bad debt.

THREE

THE FACES OF DEBT: THE GOOD, THE BAD, AND THE UGLY

Without a doubt, if you can avoid the use of any debt, do it. However, not many people have a couple hundred grand saved up to buy their first house—unless you're Donna and Steve

Houses in Connecticut are outrageously high priced. But Donna and Steve, working blue-collar jobs, saved their nickels and paid nearly $300,000 cash for their first house when they were in their late 30s. Of course, they lived with Steve's parents the entire time they were saving for the house! They sacrificed a lot to be able to pull off the debt-free home purchase—although, as the father of two small kids, I have to admit that the in-house babysitting must have been nice.

My point is that if you don't want to live with your in-laws or your parents until you're parents yourself, you may want to explore the "good debt" option of a home mortgage. By good debt I mean that it may make economic sense to acquire this type of debt. To their credit, Donna and

Steve did avoid paying $200,000 to $400,000 in
interest by paying cash for their home. Come to
think of it, their plan is sounding better by the
minute! However, the obvious benefit of taking
out a loan on a home is that you spread the payments out over time, and you get to move in before you're too old to lift your own furniture.

Because houses tend to appreciate in value,
the growth component makes a house an attrac-
tive investment. My friend Paul Aldrich, who is
an extremely funny Christian comedian from Re-
dondo Beach, California, puts it this way: "My
entire financial plan is to buy a house in California, and not die!" The way real estate has appre-
ciated on the coasts over the years, Paul's plan
has been a pretty good one—recent market cor-
rection notwithstanding. *Location* is the key to
making sure the home is a good investment.

Houses have tended to increase in value
about eight percent a year on average, plus you
get all the other tax breaks and benefits of having
your own place. You can deduct the interest payments on your taxes if you itemize on your annual return, and when you sell the property, up to
$500,000 in growth is tax free if you're married
and filing a joint return, $250,000 if you're sin-
gle. Our first house doubled in value in nine

years from the time we bought it to when we tearfully parted ways. It was such a great house! We happened to buy in a suburb of Kansas City that had the highest home-value growth rate over that time period. Location, location, location. Taking out a loan on that house turned out to be the single best investment I ever made. It proved to be very *good debt,* economically speaking. Grandma and Grandpa were always welcome to come for a visit instead of being live-in babysitters.

Good Debt to Bad

In recent years, however, the downside of the housing market has reared its ugly head, so some caution is called for. A mortgage makes financial sense if you have the cash flow to handle the huge responsibility of owning a home. You must also buy the right mortgage product. The questionable lending practices of some banks and mortgage companies caused the economy to take a nosedive and rattled the financial markets.

Three lending strategies made money for the banks and mortgage companies but quickly turned the potential of a mortgage to go from economically good debt to ghastly debt. Mortgages were extended to people who would not normally qualify due to bad credit history; these are called sub-prime loans. When those unfortunate folks fulfilled their own prophecy and proved why their credit history was bad, they defaulted on their loans, sending painful ripples through the entire economy. Further, adjustable-rate mortgages were also commonplace, allowing people to buy more house than they could really afford. When interest rates began to climb in 2006 and 2007, foreclosures spiked when people could no longer pay their higher house payments.

Finally, negative equity loans were also the rage, allowing people to borrow more money than their new house was worth. They bought a house valued at $175,000, took out a loan for $215,000, and paid off those pesky credit cards. It never occurred to them that their houses might *not* appreciate in value, that they could get laid off, that they might run the balances back up on their credit cards, or that any of a gazillion different emergencies might occur—or all of them at once. It's a commonly held belief that there are two certainties in life—death and taxes—but the reality is that there is at least one more: you'll encounter some type of emergency sooner or later that is going to cost a substantial sum of money you hadn't counted on spending.

Two weeks after we had our furnace serviced this past fall, the electronic board doohickey that makes all the furnace things happen at the right time gave up the ghost. The new thingamabob cost $453 and came right on the heels of the $160 we paid to have the furnace serviced. I love Larry the furnace guy, but I have to admit I was not too thrilled to see him again so soon. Luckily, I had a credit card to charge the thingamabob to. Just kidding! We tapped our emergency fund. We had been saving up a little bit of money each month to cover just such a repair. Trust me—emergencies will come.

There's no shortage of issues that could make a negative equity loan quickly spiral into the home-buying nightmare of all time. Sub-prime loans, adjustable-rate mortgages of less than five years, and negative equity loans are pitfalls to avoid like the bubonic plague. Going into debt to buy a house may make good economic sense if you've done your homework on a good location, purchased the loan from a reputable mortgage lender, have sufficient cash flow to make the monthly payments and potentially higher living expenses, and have additional funds in savings to cover the repair and upkeep costs that come with home ownership.

The Business of Debt

Another type of debt that may be considered good from an economic standpoint is acquiring a loan to start a business. However, like all debts, this type of debt also falls under the "Danger, Will Robinson!" clause. It has been well documented by the United States Small Business Administration that two-thirds of all businesses fail within two years.[1]

Remember my two friends who paid off all their non-mortgage debt within a few weeks of each other? They both had significant amounts of business debt that contributed to their debt-reduction plans. Running a small business is very challenging, and many of you should heed the warning: "Don't try this at home." You must have an airtight business plan that will allow you to generate enough cash flow to pay off the loan, pay your salary, meet all business expenses, cover the payroll for any other employees, and have enough to reinvest in the business. Daunting, to be sure.

I was recently talking with a friend who started his own specialty financial services company. Because of the unique nature of their product, they have some excellent prospects for strong clients and steady revenue streams. However, strain in his voice over the upper six-figure debt he and his partners had taken on was palpable. This is one of the smartest and most talented men I know. Yet even he was surprised at the effect of the debt. The complexity and enormity of launching this enterprise mushroomed when he looked at all those zeros behind his business debt total, and he has as good a chance as any to succeed. If you have a great business plan, it may make sense to take on debt of this nature, but don't embark on this journey lightly.

Degrees of Debt

Would you be interested in making a million dollars in four years? Who wouldn't? However, while you'll enjoy a lot of extra zeros in your salary, the extra cash won't come as quickly as you might be hoping for. In addition, during the four years I'm talking about there will be a lot of work—and for the next 40 years to come. Still interested?

The way to make this extra million is to go to college. According to *Spirit* magazine,[2] the average estimated lifetime earnings of a college graduate will be more than one million dollars more than a person who earns a high school diploma. That makes the cost of a college education a pretty good investment, but you still must find a way to pay for it. The final type of debt that might make good economic sense is the student loan.

The critical factor with taking on debt to work on a bachelor's degree or to improve skills or qualifications in any way, for that matter, is that the amount of debt needs to match up with the degree program one is pursuing. I often run into well-meaning scholars—or their parents— who take on nearly six figures in debt while attending a private school. While my young friends are attending fine institutions and are receiving top-quality educations, they're taking on massive debt while planning to be pastors, teachers, or missionaries—not exactly glamorous professions that pay big bucks.

I'm in no way against attending a private Christian college. I graduated from one myself, and it was a good experience that provided a great education and a valuable degree. I do think, though, that a lot of thought and prayer should go into the college selection and college funding process if you're fairly certain you or your child will enter a service field that tends to have lower-than-average wages. The amount of debt you take on has to match the future earning potential of the student. That can be pretty tricky to determine when you're sending a fresh-faced 18-year-old to God Tech. Two-thirds of traditional students require loan assistance, and the average student walks away with nearly $20,000 in student loan debt.[3] The sooner you can start praying and planning, the better.

Ben, the son of a pastor in Pennsylvania, was planning on attending an excellent Christian college in Tennessee, and he was in line to receive the president's scholarship. The full ride would be worth around $100,000 for four years of schooling. Surprisingly, Ben did not receive the award. Disappointed at this turn of events, he was relegated to taking on the six-figure debt load if he wanted to attend the Tennessee college he had planned on going to. Although the family did not have much money saved up for his schooling, his wise dad gave him a different kind of gift. Ben's dad, in true pastoral fashion, suggested that he and his son take a week to pray about his college decision in light of the sizeable debt amount they were now facing.

In a way that only God can work, during the week of prayer, the young man was contacted by another Christian college in Mississippi that he had shown some interest in. That school offered Ben its president's full-ride scholarship, and the

Lord provided in a remarkable way. Ben and his family avoided a debt load that would have strapped them for years. More important, within the first two weeks on campus Ben met his future wife, and they're happily married today.

This is a dramatic example, but what I like about this true story is not that prayer automatically leads to a huge financial blessing every time. That's not always the case. What I like about it, other than the fact that he got the girl (I know—it's so sappy) is that instead of rushing ahead and taking on a lot of debt, this family sought the Lord about the right lifestyle choice for Ben.

If you know that serving on the mission field is the student's destiny, whether the student is you or your child, then if the funds have not been saved up to cover the costs at your favorite school, perhaps attending a good junior college for a couple years to complete the core course work would be a better route. It will certainly save a bundle and still afford a good education. Community colleges offer quality alternatives and may be better money management if the long-range income projection of the student is modest.

The Lord may call you or your kids to a certain school, and you may have to take on some debt to go there. If that's where the Lord leads, then it's obviously a good thing, and you should follow His call with passion and obedience. But recognize that God may have other plans that will enable you to accomplish the same educational and vocational goals without the burden of debt. I often see the pain as people struggle to pay off their mountain of student debt, so I encourage you to pray through every option to see where the Lord leads you. An astonishing blessing may be waiting for you.

My wife desperately wanted to get into occupational therapy through the University of Kansas Medical Center. She was crushed when she received a rejection letter in reply to her application. We had prayed so much about it, but what happened next was better—much better. Out of the blue—to this day, we still don't really know how they got her name—a school serving kids with special educational needs called Cynthia and asked her to serve as a long-term substitute. On the heels of her disappointment, this offer was intriguing, because her first degree was in education. However, when she graduated the first time, the job market for teachers was extremely tight, and she had never been able to find work in her field. We sensed this phone call signaled a door was opening, and she accepted the nine-month assignment.

We saved every penny she earned from her job as a special education teacher, and she reapplied for occupational therapy school. The added experience of working with children with special needs greatly strengthened her application to an extremely competitive therapy program. The next year she was accepted into the program, and the funds needed to pay for her second degree were in the bank before her first day of class. God provided in an unexpected and wonderful way.

Generally speaking, taking on debt to enhance your education is a wise investment in your future earning potential. However, even if you don't get the girl—or guy—make sure your vocational plans are in line with the total debt load you take on to acquire your education. I would recommend taking on no more debt for college than you can reasonably earn in one year after graduation. If you're studying to be a doctor, you'll likely earn six figures, and more debt is manageable and necessary due to the demands of the training. If you're going to be a teacher earning $28,000 a year to start with, I would try to take an even more conservative approach, knowing that advancement and raise potential will be limited in your field.

Bad Debt

There's an old Hebrew saying that you must often accept both the bitter and sweet in life, as both are surely to come. We have explored debt that can make economic sense, but now we turn our attention to debt that should be avoided at all costs. The key rule of thumb in dealing with the bad-debt category is to avoid going into debt for any consumptive or depreciating items. While using credit cards and not paying them off each month is the obvious culprit, there are several other types of bad debt.

If you're considering using your credit card to purchase food, clothes, computers, restaurant meals, haircuts, a cell phone, or anything you can buy in a retail store, and you don't intend to pay your bill off at the end of the month, it's a bad debt. Don't do it. Run for your life.

Look at it this way: would you go out and buy any consumer item and try to find a deal where you can pay between ten and twenty-eight percent more than the list price? I didn't think so. The future pain is never worth the immediate gain, no matter what the advertisement tells you, if you can't pay your full credit card balance each month.

I know—it's convenient. Shop, choose, swipe, enjoy today, pay later! No waiting. The same temptations existed during Jesus' day. He said, "Watch out! Be on your guard for all kinds of greed; a man's life does not consist in the abundance of his possessions" (Luke 12:15). The dangers of credit cards leading people into debt have been well documented. No need to rehash it. What's critical is to heed Jesus' warning, or the sequence will end up like this: Shop, choose, swipe, enjoy today, and suffer pain later—and pay a lot more for it. Are you on your guard? Are you handling your financial affairs with caution so that you can avoid materialism and bad debt?

Upside Down

Car loans also fall into the bad debt category, because cars depreciate faster than greased lightning. Your new $40,000 sport utility gas guzzler will lose about 15 percent of its value the day you drive it off the lot. If you take out a sizable loan, let's say more than $15,000, you can quickly owe more on the car than it's worth. It's called being upside down on your loan.

One of the best ways to straighten out your finances is to drive the car you own for about 15 years—or more. Even 12 years would be about seven years longer than the national average.

Cars are not cash-eaters—they're cash devourers! Avoiding the auto trap is one of the most powerful financial moves you can make. Don't fall for the following arguments for buying a new car:

The car is no longer under warranty. Better get a new one! Save up money for some repairs and routine maintenance. This will be a lot more affordable than a monthly payment.

The car needs expensive repairs. Better get a new one! This point can be argued if the car is worth less than the amount of the repairs. You could still be far ahead, though, if you can get another year out of it.

We've driven this car for almost five years. We deserve a newer model. This argument usually means you "greatly desire" a new one. Deserve a new one? That's a slippery slope. The buzz of the new car lasts about a week—maximum. Go to the showroom and sit in this year's model, breath the new car smell, and then go home and thank the Lord that you don't have a car payment due next month.

This car gets bad gas mileage, and gas keeps going up. Better get a new one! Even with the shockingly high price of gas these days, it would take a massive difference in your fuel consumption to justify the expense of a new vehicle.

Resisting the temptation to burn money on cars has been one of the key strategies for helping our family maintain biblical financial success. My wife and I have never earned huge sums of money, but we have no debt except for our mortgage. We live within our means, and we've saved regularly. Most important, we've not paid interest on a car loan since 1996. We paid that car off in half the time, and that's the only time we've ever paid interest on a car. Once it was paid off, we drove it for another 13½ years.

You can do this too. It may take you a year or so to work into this strategy. You may have a jalopy on its last leg that you still owe on, and there's no amount of duct tape that will keep it going for 12 or 15 years. Fair enough. But make sure the next car you buy is one of the top three makes for reliability. According to *Consumer Reports*, those are currently Honda, Subaru, and Toyota.[4] Also, start saving money now for that next reliable, boring, used car that won't come at the price of your financial future.

Don't despair if you already have a car loan. It's best to avoid it, but I know that getting to work or school are high priorities. See my book *Managing Your Money*, also published by Beacon Hill Press of Kansas City, for strategies on avoiding car loans and buying good used cars. If it's necessary to have one or the other, it's much better to have a car loan than credit card debt. In time, as you follow biblical principles for managing the money God has given you, you'll be free from all consumer and auto debt. As you work toward that end, a car loan is generally much easier to manage and avoid in the future and will cost potentially thousands less in interest payments. Once your credit card debt is paid off, then work on a car loan strategy. Take small steps, and you'll be debt free in no time.

The Ugly Debt

After examining the good debt and the bad debt, we must address ugly debt. This is the worst of the lot and is so bad that *ugly* is too kind a label for it. In the ugly debt category are (1) home equity loans for debt consolidation and (2) payday loans. These major debt traps lurk in the financial jungle and have the potential to cripple you financially at alarming rates. As if credit card debt isn't bad enough!

In more than a decade of being a financial coach, I've had one family come to me for assistance who actually used their second mortgage to fix up their home. One! Every other family has used the second mortgage to consolidate debts. I know it sounds like a wise strategy to lower your payments and take advantage of tax-deductible interest. But placing your most important asset, your home, on the line when you've had a history of misusing credit cards is riskier than taking your retirement savings to Vegas. The chance of running the credit cards back up, not being able to make both mortgage payments, and losing your house is far too great. The pain it would cause is far too devastating. I've seen it happen, and it's not pretty. Don't run the risk of foreclosure. Follow my get-out-of-debt plan in chapter 5 instead.

Payday loans—or the new politically correct and more deceptive name *cash advances*—are perhaps the most despicable of all financial debt tools. These small, short-term loans of usually $500 or less carry annualized interest rates of up to 780 percent, depending on how long you hold the loan. A typical amount would be 391 percent annualized interest for a two-week loan. If you needed some quick cash for that "unexpected" emergency (nudge, nudge, wink, wink) and went to a payday loan provider for a $200 loan, you would need to pay back $230 in 14 days. And this is advertised as a low-fee, low-interest loan![5] I guess they expect you to be grateful they didn't sell you the *high*-interest, *high*-fee loan! That one would have been murder.

The outrageous interest amounts charged on these kinds of loans should be illegal. God's Word sheds some interesting light on this topic in Proverbs 28:8—"He who increases his wealth by exorbitant interest amasses it for another, who will be kind to the poor." Traditionally, payday loan providers have preyed on the poor, which is really quite ironic in light of the fact that eventually the Lord says all their profits will end up helping the poor. That day cannot come too soon. Come quickly, Lord, and make it so.

Can you believe that the advertising materials for the payday loan centers claim there are no hidden fees with these types of loans? *Of course* there are no hidden fees! Why would they need a hidden fee when they're ripping you off and robbing you blind in broad daylight with the *posted* fees? With this kind of arrangement, it's hard to imagine it could get any worse, but now payday loans are available even online. A cash advance store has seemingly sprung up in every strip mall in America in recent years, so be on your guard. The devil is definitely prowling about looking for someone to devour.

We've seen there are several types of debt that

may make economic sense to take on, such as a mortgage or school loan. These types of debt have the potential to improve your financial situation over time by either increasing your earning potential or by the appreciating value of your home. Of course, you still need to exercise caution with any type of debt and ensure that you have sufficient cash flow to cover the payments and meet your other obligations. Conversely, there are plenty of bad debt options out there that are very easy to get into and extremely difficult to get out of.

As we explore in the next chapter what the Bible has to say about debt, we'll see how debt can often lead us down a dangerous path. We hear many messages in our culture telling us how to get rich quickly, but we rarely hear warnings that bad debt can result in getting *poor* quickly!

FOUR

THE BIBLE AND DEBT

The Bible's approach to debt would probably be considered old fashioned by today's standards. But its teachings on saving little by little, working hard, planning for the future, and using debt responsibly are still the key ingredients to financial well-being. The recent wave of easy credit, sub-prime mortgages, and the explosion of cash advance services are seducing consumers away from sound thinking and wise decisions. Let's look at three key teachings from the Bible concerning debt for a firm understanding of God's view of borrowing.

No debt is the best debt, of course. When you're 100-percent debt free, including for your cars and mortgage, you're in a unique position of power not only financially—although those benefits are important—but also spiritually. When you're truly debt free, you're free to do whatever God calls you to do whenever He calls you to do it. Can you imagine what might have happened if Abraham had racked up a couple thousand shekels of debt? "Lord, Canaan sounds really swell, and I'd love to check it out—just as soon as I can pay off a few bills. Check with me in a couple years, and I'll see if we can swing that trip." If Abraham had not been financially sound and saved up a strong supply of resources, he would not have been able to answer the call.

The Bible does not prohibit us from taking on debt, but a number of passages direct us to be especially cautious and responsible when dealing with it. Proverbs 22:6-8 is a revealing passage as it relates to debt and our ability to freely serve God: "Train a child in the way he should go, and when he is old he will not turn from it. The rich rule over the poor, and the borrower is servant to the lender. He who sows wickedness reaps trouble, and the rod of his fury will be destroyed." The first two verses in this passage are both fairly familiar, but you may be surprised, as I was, to realize they were paired together.

We often gain greater insight into scripture when we look at the surrounding verses. Part of the training we give our children should be to educate them on the power of debt and how it can lead them into servitude. If we teach our kids the way they should go, they'll find greater freedom in their finances and their spiritual lives by avoiding most kinds of debt. The implication is that you'll reap less trouble if you're not in bondage to debt. And like my allusion to Abraham, when we're completely debt free, we're in a much better position to serve God any way He leads us. This is the ultimate wisdom when it comes to managing debt.

A second passage from the New Testament reveals another key theme about debt. Romans 13:8 provides a straightforward teaching about debt—pay it off. "Let no debt remain outstanding, except the continuing debt to love one another, for he who loves his fellowman has fulfilled the law." This verse leads us to do the loving thing with our money, which includes paying back our debts. In this passage, in which Paul instructs believers to be responsible, submit to authority, and put on the nature of Christ, he also makes known his assumption that some of God's people will have debts. His emphasis is not that we should have no debt. Rather, we need to show the love of Christ to everyone, including our creditors, by paying them back and paying them on time. Showing love to others, even if they maintain power over us financially or governmentally, demonstrates that we're living out the key element of Christianity: to love like Jesus.

In Psalm 37:21 is found an even stronger ex-
hortation to pay back our debts: "The wicked
borrow and do not repay, but the righteous give
generously." This verse combines the concepts of
debt and giving. If we focus our hearts on giving,
we can avoid the bondage of debt, and our God-
like righteousness will reflect the love of our Father. However, if we have the capability but don't
pay back our debts, we exhibit wicked and sinful
behavior. Paying our debts on time should be a
high priority to help us maintain spiritual health
and a positive witness.

The final broad theme in the Bible about debt
instructs us to treat others fairly if they're in debt
to us. This reinforces the idea that debt is not
prohibited, but our focus should be to take a loving approach in both paying our creditors on
time and not charging excessive interest if we're
the creditor. "You may charge a foreigner interest, but not a brother Israelite, so that the Lord
your God may bless you in everything you put
your hand to in the land you are entering to pos-
sess" (Deuteronomy 23:20).

It's okay to charge reasonable interest to those
who are engaged in trade or commerce and need
a loan. To neighbors and family, fellow Israelites,
who needed funds for the basic needs of life, no

interest was to be levied. Mirroring the justice,
love, and mercy of the Lord, one did not put a
brother at an economic disadvantage because he
had a bad crop or some other setback. Integrity
and lovingkindness reigned supreme, and they're
worthy goals for our financial dealings with others.

Exodus 22:25 expands on the theme of righteous lending: "If you lend money to one of my
people among you who is needy, do not be like a
moneylender; charge him no interest." I think
this is telling us that God's people should do debt
differently. We should be more concerned with
caring for the poor, showing love to others, and
conducting our business affairs with integrity.
It's clear that it's all right to make money through
lending, but the primary issue is to focus on
faithfulness—our faithfulness to ministering to
the poor and those in need.

The Bible's broad brush strokes on borrowing
teach us to respect God's money and handle it
wisely, be cautious with debt, pay back our creditors in a timely manner, and treat others who
may borrow from us with fairness, remembering
first and foremost to show special consideration
to the poor. This is a winning and biblical formu-
la for approaching debt. This inspiration from

God's Word, combined with common sense, enables us to live out the Scriptures, pay off our debts, and show love to others.

FIVE

THE 10-STEP PLAN TO SHRINK YOUR DEBT: STEPS 1-6

"Get out of debt in 90 minutes without borrow-ing!" This advertisement in a weekly ad pack is one of my favorites. There was even a coupon for free financial advice. You may be thinking, *Nine-ty minutes! If I'm out of debt in ninety minutes, I can be at the mall in under two hours!*

Not surprisingly, there were no real details of how this miraculous 90-minute plan would work to alleviate all your debt. But it surely sounds al-luring—so very tempting.

The reality is that you're probably very tired of the stress and the strain of trying to dig out from under your debts, so tired that you might be tempted to grasp that 90-minute solution. That's understandable. Dealing with unrelenting debt is exhausting. Getting into debt was so easy. The sign-up was easy, purchasing the stuff was easy, but finding the money to pay off the debt— not so much.

Guess what. You don't need one of those quick-fix solutions, which are really no solution at all. You're one of God's children; you can succeed in your debt-reduction plan with His help.

It will take more than 90 minutes to get out of debt, but we're going to look at 10 steps to becoming debt free that will really work.

The 10-Step Get-Out-of-Debt Plan

Step 1: Take on no new debt. Period.

There's no leeway in the first step. You can bail water for all you're worth from a boat that's sinking, but you'll never save the vessel if water continues to pour in from a gash in the hull.

You must employ self-control and commit to a money management system that does not use incurring more debt as a strategy for paying the bills. (See *Managing Your Money*, my first book in this series, for information on setting up your simple and effective money management system.)

Step 2: Establish a spending plan.

Once you commit to a different financial path, it will be important to set up your spending plan. A spending plan, when used as designed, will provide you with a flexible and real-world financial management tool that will lead you to success in your debt-reduction plan.

A spending plan differs from a typical budget in several ways. First, most budgets consist of some numbers scribbled down on a piece of paper. Usually people will write out how much money they think they'll earn and how much they think they'll spend in a month. Unfortunately, that's often their only step in the plan. The problems with this are (1) The numbers on the page that you have projected for income and expenses may have no correlation to what actually happens in your household on any given month. It does not give you a true picture of reality— how much is *really* being earned and where the money is *really* going. (2) A traditional budget provides no flexibility for changes in the plan. Every month I set a projection of our income and expenses, but I don't think there's ever been a month when every expense category came in exactly as planned. Does that mean we should not set a plan? No, it means we need a more realistic and flexible tool than a budget. (3) Traditional budgets don't allow for mid-month modifications. Even if you track your expenses each month, it can be less than helpful if you're not using the information to help you stay on track.

A few years back, I met a woman who was doing an out-of-this-world job at writing down where she and her husband spent their money each month. She had reams of books, charts, and tracking tools that she brought to our coaching session. She could tell me to the penny where they spent their money. But she still found herself needing some financial coaching.

There was a problem with her system: she never did expense-tracking until *after* the month was over. On the third or fourth of the next month, when she tallied the expenditures, she would say, "Wow—we spent more than we made again!" Even if you track your expenses, it won't help you if you don't at some point during the month compare your spending to your income.

A true spending plan will allow you to get over these money management and planning hurdles so that you can live within your means and pay off your debts. Following the Abundant Living spending plan that we teach in our workshops will allow you to set monthly targets for income and expenses, track where you're spending your money, and give you a simple tool to access your spending as you work through the month. This will allow you the flexibility of shifting funds from one spending category to another while meeting the most important goal of spending less than you make each month. (You can learn to set up your spending plan in _Managing Your Money,_ my first book in this series, or go to <www.abundantlivingministry.org>.)

Step 3: Discard your credit cards.

Earlier I said that the real issue here is self-control rather than the use of plastic. While I believe that holds true, when you're in debt-reduction mode, getting the credit cards out of your hands will be an important step in making your plan successful. The last thing you need is a plastic rectangle calling your name if you've been struggling with out-of-control use of credit.

If you have more than two credit cards, set aside the two with the lowest interest rates and cut up the remaining cards. You'll need to check your statements to determine your interest rates. Make sure the remaining two cards are not in your possession—or your spouse's possession if you're married. Lock the cards in a safe deposit box at the bank, or give them to a trusted friend or advisor who will keep them in a safe and secure place. You do not want easy access to the cards. Make it very difficult and painful for you to even think about using those credit cards.

You may wonder why I didn't suggest cutting them _all_ up. The reason is that most people in serious debt-reduction mode will not have cash set aside in an emergency fund. When the inevitable emergency rudely intrudes on your diligent debt reduction, how will you pay for it? You might be able to sell something of value to generate some quick cash, but that strategy is not always a given. You could borrow from a retirement plan if you're fortunate enough be part of a plan that offers loans. All things considered, it's better to borrow from yourself and your 401(k) plan. You'll at least be able to pay yourself back with interest.

Therefore, you may have a legitimate need to use a credit card at some point in the future if you have no other options. That's why you should keep one or two cards that have no annual fee and that carry the lowest interest rates. That's better than getting a payday loan and forking out an obscenely high interest rate to fix the brakes on the car! It's important that you not keep the card in your possession. If the card is held by a trusted friend or advisor, you'll need to convince him or her that you have a true emergency that requires you to take on more debt. A 75-percent-off sale at the department store is not a true emergency.

If you can cut all your cards up and still get through emergency situations, that's even better.

Nevertheless, I would rather you increase your credit card balance than do something rash such as getting a payday loan.

Step 4: Make a list of all your debt.

A list of all your debt will include all your past-due debts. It will not include rent or utilities, but do include amounts for any bills you're behind on by more than 30 days.

It's critical that you include three pieces of information on your list: (1) the total owed for each debt (2) the rate of interest you're paying on each debt (Even if there's 0-percent interest on your debt for the time being, include it on the list.) and (3) the minimum payment you must make each month on the debt. This information is important so that you can formulate your personalized debt-reduction plan, figure out what debts to attack first, and determine how much you're going to pay on each one. It will probably take you at least an hour to pull all this information together. See the appendix at the end of this book for some help in building your plan. Don't worry if it's not perfect—just do your best to capture the key data mentioned here. Knowing the interest rates is the most important of all. If you can't find the information, call your creditors to get the most recent data.

Step 5: Sell assets, if possible, and put that money toward debt repayment.

What do an ATV, women's clothes, and a car have in common? They all were sold to help supercharge the debt-reduction plans of people who have received help from the Abundant Living personal finance training ministry. One young man who came to our workshops had around $8,000 of credit card debt. He also had a super-cool, show version, all-terrain vehicle (ATV). When push came to shove, he realized he didn't really need the ATV, so he sold it, paid off all his credit cards, and overnight he was out from under his burden of debt. That was a rare and wonderful debt-reduction story.

Another young lady had more than $800 worth of clothes in her closet with the tags still on them. She had never worn any of the items. She returned them to the department store, got her money back, and made a nice dent in her credit card bill. A third family, a married couple, had three cars after their last child moved out of the nest. They sold one and paid down a nice portion on their cards.

Look around your house or apartment. See if you have some items of value that you don't really need or want. You may be surprised by what you find, and it's worth the small effort to gain a powerful jumpstart to your debt-reduction plan. Becoming aware of how much you have that you don't need may also have the side benefit of aiding you in your fight against materialism. Unloading some of your stuff may help you focus on that which is most important: the Lord and your relationships. Gaining the joy and freedom that come by eliminating your debt far outweighs any satisfaction you get from things.

Step 6: Establish a repayment plan with your creditors.

Once you've identified all the debt you owe in Step 4, and hopefully paid the balance down by at least a few extra bucks using Step 5, it's time to do business with your creditors. Your goal is to get your interest rates lowered and your payments reduced. This may seem a bit scary or unattainable, but it's the step that can save you some big bucks over the course of what will likely be a multi-year debt-reduction plan.

Your objective is to work out a repayment plan with your creditors. It will probably take several hours and a few phone calls to the credit card companies, so it will also let you practice exhibiting the Holy Spirit fruit of patience and love. Remember: the folks on the other end of the phone are just doing their jobs. Be kind and courteous, but also be firm and resolute. Here's a list of a few things you should do to prepare:

1. Make sure you have a copy of your spending plan and a list of your debts to share with your creditors. Be prepared to fax or e-mail a copy to each creditor you contact. Remember: your goal is to work with them to reduce your interest rates and payments. Sharing this information will show them that you're serious about paying them. Let them know you have a workable plan, but you want reasonable repayment amounts based on your real income and expenses so that you can be successful. You might remind them that they are the ones who extended you enough credit rope to hang yourself with, so they are partially culpable. Admit your part as well, but try to stick to the facts and save the sob stories. They've heard it all before

2. Once on the phone, immediately ask for a manager. Customer service reps are people, too; however, they're usually people with no authority to make a decision. I save my breath and work only with managers. The customer service reps are probably trained to do everything in their power to keep you from talking to the manager or supervisor. Using your cool,

calm, and friendly demeanor, stick to your guns and refuse to take no for an answer.

3. Be prepared. Tell them your plan for paying them back. Practice what you're going to say. This may be nerve-wracking or emotional, especially if the creditors become confrontational or are unhelpful. Get your spiel down before you call, and it should go more smoothly. If needed, ask a friend to be there with you for moral support.

4. After making your case, ask to have your interest rates reduced. Generally, you won't get the rate below 10 percent. However, if you're currently at 15 or 20 percent or more, this reduction will save you hundreds, if not thousands, of dollars as you repay your loans. Recently a couple at my workshop in San Francisco examined their credit card statement and found that their interest rate was a whopping 31 percent on that credit card. After I shared this strategy with the group, the wife left the seminar while we were still in session, called the card company, and their interest rate was immediately reduced to 8.99 percent. I've never seen a smile so big as when she came bounding back into the seminar to tell us the good news! Another couple called the

holder of their auto loan, and their rate was reduced by 2 percent with no paperwork. Give it a try—it won't make things any worse, and it could make things a whole lot better.

5. Remember: everything is negotiable. Have some cash right now? See if they will take a settlement and call it even. It's worth a shot. If you owe $5,000, offer them $3,000, and see what they say. Make sure you get any agreement in writing on their letterhead.

More than anything, the lender wants your interest dollars. When faced with the prospect of losing your business, they'll often reduce your rates to keep your loan. Suggest that you're going to transfer the balance to another credit card or obtain an alternate loan from a different lender. Gently remind them that they'll lose your interest dollars if you bolt for another lender. This is not lying—this is negotiating. Making that move is always open to you, and you can call some other card companies or lenders to give you the ammo you need for your conversations.

If they absolutely will not budge on dropping your rates, don't give up on the get-out-of-debt plan and say, "See—I knew it wouldn't work!" This is only Step 6, and there are still four exciting debt-reduction steps to go! There's even a

Plan B for handling those creditors who won't or can't work with you.

Plan B

If you've had a lot of late payments and your credit score is in the danger zone, creditors may be unable to work with you as described above. But not all is lost. It's just time for Plan B. Your next option in trying to reduce your interest rates, and thus your payments, is to explore the use of a credit counseling service. A credit counseling service (CCS) may be your best friend if you're truly willing to change your spending habits and stop using credit cards. As with any debt-reduction plan, if you don't change your spending habits and begin living within your means, you won't achieve success. If you're able to negotiate lower rates on your own, that route is always your best bet.

A CCS allows you to consolidate all your debt payments into one payment that will be made directly to the CCS. They take your payment and pay all your creditors on a monthly basis according to your debt repayment plan. Also, the CCS negotiates with the creditors on your behalf to stop phone calls regarding late payments, lower your rates (again, usually to 10 percent), reduce fees, and lower your monthly payments. These

counseling services have stock contracts with the
card companies that allow them to negotiate
these deals for you. If managed correctly, and if
you stick with the plan to take on no new debt,
you'll take giant steps toward financial peace in
Christ.

If you're struggling each month to keep track
of five to ten payments to creditors, this will sim-
plify your life and streamline your bill-paying by
making only one payment to the CCS, and the
lower payments will allow you to focus on your
plan and generate more money to go toward
debt relief. Additionally, the lower interest rates
will save you major dollars and help you get out
of debt faster. Can you feel the positive momentum flowing in your direction?

You'll be required to pay a set-up fee to get
the process going (usually $25 to $100), and
you'll also pay a monthly maintenance fee for the
CCS to handle paying your creditors (it also
ranges from $25 to $100 monthly depending on
the company). Sorry—no free lunch here; however, if your interest rates drop from the 20-percent
range to 10 percent, the monthly maintenance
fee will be the best $25 dollars you spend each
month, because it will save you so much money
on interest payments in the long run.

Now for the downside. There are two potential problems with using a CCS. First, there are many unscrupulous credit counseling services out there, so you should be very careful in selecting which one will help you with your debt management plan. To help you make a wise choice, the Abundant Living ministry has partnered with A Safe Harbor Credit Management, a Christian-owned CCS helping clients nationwide (<www.40debts.org>). Obviously many other firms exist that offer these services, and you can check with the Better Business Bureau of the city in which the CCS is located, conduct a thorough online search for other reputable companies, or contact the National Foundation for Credit Counseling for a referral (<www.nfcc.org>).

Second, use of a CCS may lower your credit rating initially. However, I would not be overly alarmed by this. A Safe Harbor Credit Management explains it this way:

> If you have poor credit when joining a debt management program, your credit rating will actually improve after the first year of consistent payments. When you become active on any debt management plan, creditors may place a "CC" [for "credit counseling"] on your credit report, signifying "slow pay." Ini-

tially, this rating could present a derogatory impact should you need to acquire a loan. However, most creditors appreciate the fact that you have the integrity and discipline to establish a payment plan.[1]

Assuming you stick with the plan, the result of using a CCS will be an improved credit score over time by eliminating late payments and creating a regular stream of on-time payments—the number-one factor in improving your credit score, according to Fair Isaac Company, creator of the FICO credit score. If you've been struggling to pay your bills on time and have racked up some serious debt, the odds are that your credit score is in need of some mouth-to-mouth resuscitation anyway. A CCS may be what you need for a fresh start and a workable debt management plan.

Let's move on to the next four steps to help you shrink your debt.

SIX

THE 10-STEP PLAN TO SHRINK YOUR DEBT: STEPS 7-10

Let's do a quick review of the first six steps to shrink your debt:

Step 1: Take on no new debt. Period.

Step 2: Establish a spending plan.

Step 3: Discard your credit cards.

Step 4: Make a list of all your debt.

Step 5: Sell assets if possible, and put that money toward debt repayment.

Step 6: Establish a repayment plan with your creditors.

Now on to Step 7 in your 10-step plan.

Step 7: Organize, set the priorities of your debt-reduction plan, and get started.

Grab the list of your debts that you compiled in Step 4. In order to pay off your debts as quickly as possible and save the most money on interest, you'll organize and set the priorities of your debt repayment plan. In the appendix you'll find a worksheet for completing your plan. From your original list you'll compile your personalized debt-reduction plan, or you can use the worksheet.

As you begin, look at your original list of debts and choose the smallest debt with the highest interest rate. This debt will be first on your new list. Include the interest rate and your minimum payment amount. Next, choose the largest debt with the highest interest rate, and put it second on your list, including the interest rate and minimum payment. Continue this pattern of putting in the largest debt with the highest interest rate and the amount of the minimum payment in descending order until you've listed all your debts.

You understand by now that paying the minimum amount due on these balances will never retire them. So to the first debt on your new list, determine an additional amount of money you can pay on that debt every single month without fail. It may be only $50 or $100. Obviously, the more you commit to paying on this first debt, the faster the balance will shrink. But you must come up with an extra amount to pay on this debt. This is why your spending plan is critical. It can help you identify where you can free up extra money to pay down this debt, track your expenses, keep you living within your means, and help you manage the resources the Lord has given you.

It's also critical that you continue to pay the minimum amount due on your other debts each month, paying extra dollars only on the first debt on your list.

A common mistake I see is that people in debt-reduction mode will get a little extra cash, and instead of applying it to the debt at the top of their list, they'll pay off a little bit on each debt. While this strategy does reduce each balance, it does not affect the debt with the highest interest rate, which is draining the most from your finances. If you get a bonus at work or a gift from a family member, apply it to the top debt on your list, and continue paying the agreed-upon debt reduction amount faithfully each month. Be sure when sending in extra payments to designate them for reduction of principal so that they don't get applied to your account as a regular payment.

Take a look at the sample debt reduction plan in this chapter. Notice that after totaling the minimum payments and the extra amount paid toward the Visa debt at the top of the list, the total debt payment for the month is $554. This is the amount you'll be paying on debt reduction every

single month until every debt on the list is re-
tired.

Don't give in to the temptation to try to pay
more one month and then cut back in December
because it's Christmas. Stay consistent, and pay
this amount every month until you're free of
debt. The only exception would be if you receive
a lump-sum windfall of some sort as we previously mentioned.

The number-one way to get derailed from
your debt-reduction plan is to jump all over the
map with your monthly repayment amounts. Remember: stick with your systematic plan. Paying
the same amount each month breeds consistency, and consistency breeds success.

Sample Debt-Reduction Plan

Debt	Balance	Interest Rate	Monthly Payment	Extra Payment	Total Monthly Payment
Visa	$260	14%	$10	$75	$85
Elec. store	$3,678	24%	$150		$150
MC	$1,950	22%	$39		$39
Disc.	$2,976	15%	$119		$119
Car	$5,796	8%	$161		$161
Total	$14,660		$479	$75	$554

You may wonder why I show the smallest
debt at the top of the list instead of the one with
the highest interest rate. This strategy allows you
to get positive momentum going as you pay off a

small debt first so that you achieve quick success as you get your plan moving. Getting that first debt paid off quickly will get you motivated to tackle the bigger ones.

Step 8: Now that your first debt is paid off, apply that monthly payment to the second debt on your list.

As tempting as it might be to take that $85 you've been applying to your first debt and go out to eat, refrain yourself and practice that self-control we've been talking about. Hold on just a little longer. We'll talk about rewards in Step 9.

You're going to take that $85 per month and apply it to the next debt on the list. In the sample, that's the $3,678 owed to the electronics store.

As you continue to follow this pattern of applying the newly freed-up funds to the next debt on your list, you'll be debt free in approximately two years and seven months; you'll even be free of car payments! You may want to consider taking your $554 and building a savings fund for emergencies and your next car purchase.

Let's assume your car is five years old when your debt is behind you, and you drive it for five more years. If you put $250 each month into a savings fund, you will have $15,000 saved up for your next automobile. If you put the other $200 per month into an emergency fund, you'll have more than $12,000 in your funds for a rainy day.

In just 10 years you can go from more than $14,000 of debt to more than $27,000 in savings!

There is a good reason people use systems like this one: they work. If you invest a portion of the surplus into a conservative mutual fund, you may be in an even stronger position to take care of yourself and your family. Don't forget the Lord's part in your money management success. A generous gift to ministry to thank Him for helping you get out of debt would be a spiritually powerful way to leave a lasting legacy of love.

Step 8 is powerful—not easy, mind you, but powerful. It will restore you to financial health. Can you grasp the vision of being debt free? Anticipate the fruit of the Spirit—love, joy, peace, and self-control—flowing through your financial life in new and enhanced ways.

Step 9: Set up some reasonable rewards to keep you motivated and enthusiastic about your debt-reduction plan.

Identify specific rewards that will inspire you. Maybe you would be inspired by treating yourself to dinner out every time you cross a debt off your list. Use a portion of the funds you've freed up to celebrate. Maybe you could take your family out for ice cream each month you spend less than you make. Or have a latte as a reward for not using your credit cards. It's important to choose rewards that won't blow your spending plan and that are particularly meaningful to you.

A woman in Indiana who was attending our Abundant Living financial coaching program was certain her coach was going to lower the boom on her. She and her husband were in a dire situation, and she was nervous that the financial coach would notice that she had had her nails done and demand that she chop that luxury from her spending plan. But the first thing that wise coach did was to tell her that she absolutely must keep getting her nails done. He realized that this small reward was key to keeping this family's debt-reduction plan operational. As the family's primary breadwinner, she found that eating out was not important to her. Clothes didn't do much for her either. But getting her nails done was the one and only small luxury she had left to keep her going in their steep, uphill financial battle. She broke down in tears when the financial coach told her to continue having her nails done as her motivational reward. Your reward may not bring you to tears, but it should be something significant for you.

Step 10: Enlist someone to hold you accountable.

You've done a great job getting all the data organized and in place. You have a system that will work to get your debts paid off.

I previously mentioned the idea of having a financial coach to help you stay motivated while you're in debt-reduction mode. I highly recommend that you ask a friend, mentor, or trusted family member, or form a relationship with a financial coach, who can assist you as you pay off your debts.

This person should be someone who will hold you accountable for your plan, encourage you when you feel discouraged, put a thumb in your back when you're tempted to slack off the plan, and pray for you as you work through the challenges of reinventing your finances. The benefit of using a financial coach rather than a friend or family member is that he or she may be tougher on you when you need it. A friend or family member might be hesitant to speak up for fear of hurting your relationship.

Regardless, choose someone you respect who is good with finances and is willing to walk through this challenge with you. If you wish to explore using a financial coach, contact Abundant Living at <www.abundantlivingministry.org>.

This final step provides several benefits: loving help, fair accountability, and a sense of Christian community. John Wesley said, "There is no such thing as a solitary Christian." There's no advantage to bravely putting on your game face and traversing the grueling debt-reduction path alone. Just the opposite is true. When you drag your financial struggles out of the shadows and enlist the help of mature and loving followers of Jesus, you'll be strengthened and encouraged to complete all 10 of these important steps so that you can grow in Christ, be in a better position to serve Him, and show love to yourself, your family, and others through good stewardship of the resources God has given you.

SEVEN

AUTOMATICALLY DEBT FREE NOW

The two biggest mistakes I observe in people embarking on debt-reduction plans are (1) continuing to use their credit cards while trying to pay off their credit cards and (2) changing the amount they're going to pay down on debt every month. The first mistake will be corrected by following the first and second steps of the 10-step plan. The second mistake can be avoided if you automatically become debt free.

A $90,000 Mountain of Debt

This real-life illustration demonstrates the power of adopting this strategy to become automatically debt free.

Ron had a sizable debt load to tackle. He owed more than $90,000 in credit card debt, school loans, and business debt. But once he made up his mind to become debt free and asked for God's help, he became debt free automatically.

Although a large chunk of Ron's debt was

from returning to law school in his late 30s, he
quickly acknowledged to me that he too easily
accepted debt as a strategy to pay for law school.
Another non-traditional student in his class con-
tinued to work while she was in law school, and
Ron admitted that he could have kept working
himself and could have avoided a significant portion of that debt. Instead, he racked up credit
card debt for living expenses while in school and
later for start-up expenses for his business. With
his debt load rapidly approaching six figures,
Ron knew he needed to make changes fast. The
weight of his debt was dragging him down. After
a few years of struggling, paying down some
debt only to rack up more later, he launched his
new automatic debt-reduction plan.

The first thing Ron did to get his debt-reduction plan underway was automate his month-to-
month finances. Using Quicken financial software, he set up his bill-paying system on
computer, including reoccurring monthly bills
that would be automatically entered in the software package. This step, which also included setting up his spending plan, was especially helpful,
because he knew for the first time exactly where
he stood on all his debts. Keeping all the information in one place and automated on the com-

puter was a major step for him. Before he set up this system, he had no idea how much he owed.

Once he knew what he was up against, he chose an amount he was going to pay on his debts automatically every single month. He used his bank's Web site to set up what are called auto drafts. A set amount would be paid automatically each month to each creditor. Using this very structured, disciplined, and automatic approach, he paid off his credit card debt and then moved on to his school loans.

The key is that these payments were automatic. He did not have to fret each month about what he should pay each creditor—the same amount was sent monthly until a debt was paid off. Because it was automated, it was also easy to make adjustments as needed using the Web-based payment tools. There were no checks to write, stamps to lick, or envelopes to mail. He didn't have to keep track of whether or not he had paid a certain creditor, because the checks were automatically generated by his bank, paid from his checking account, mailed to his creditors, and recorded in his financial software package—automatically!

Using the 10-step plan, Ron paid off his smallest debt first, then attacked the debts carrying the highest interest rates. In only five years he wiped out $90,000 in debt on an annual average income of $45,000. The occasional bonus from work went toward paying off debt.

Ron adopted a very disciplined approach and got serious about using his spending plan. Through the use of the money management software, he planned his basic expenses well into the future. His secret was that he calculated and knew what his essential expenses would be for the next six months. Based on his keen planning, Ron knew how much he would have left over each month, and he paid every spare nickel toward his debt through the autopay system. After living for years with the sinking feeling of not knowing how much debt he had and wondering if he could pay the bills, his new approach of really focusing on his finances made a huge difference in his financial and spiritual life. The old pattern of ignoring bills for a month and then sitting down to try to write checks for $600 in bills when there was only $300 in the checking account became a thing of the past.

Using his spending plan, Ron set up level payment plans on as many bills as possible—also automatically deducted from his checking account. This smoothed out his monthly bill paying. Knowing exactly when the utility bill would be deducted from his checking account as opposed to making sure the bill got sent in on time was a big stress-reliever. Tracking it all was a snap in Quicken. He got better and better at looking ahead and setting a plan for how much he would spend.

One thing Ron did was a bit unorthodox. However, it fits with one of my main money management beliefs that you need to come up with a system that works for you. While I don't normally advise folks paying off credit cards to use credit cards, Ron's approach was so disciplined that he made his plan work.

He maintained two credit cards. All the credit card debt that he had acquired was on one card. He never added new expenditures to this card, and he followed his automatically debt-free plan by directing the monthly automatic payment from his bank to pay down the debt.

He maintained a second card through which he funneled all his month-to-month spending. This method simplified his monthly cash flow management because he had a central location for all his transactions. Writing a check became a rare occurrence.

Again, because he had a detailed spending

plan, he made sure he lived within his means, and he diligently paid off this second credit card every single month.

He also made other significant decisions that helped his automatic debt-reduction plan, starting with a fresh look at his job. He got very honest with himself and admitted that he was not the risk-taking entrepreneur that he had strived to be. A sizable portion of his debt came from business start-up costs for ventures that never panned out. The up-and-down life and inconsistent paychecks from being a small business owner took their toll. He humbled himself, got real, and realized that it would be a much better fit for his gifts and skill-set to find a job in his primary field—law. This was a key step for getting out of debt, because he realized he would never get his debt paid off unless his income was stabilized.

Instead of hoping for the big payday on some entrepreneurial business venture, he realigned his priorities with what he felt God was calling him to do. During this time he also got married. This further helped him to focus on his responsibilities and calling. His wife was a saver who further encouraged him in a debt-free lifestyle. Most important, he realized he needed to be more respectful of the resources God had provided for him.

Interestingly, Ron rarely gave himself a reward as he paid off his debt. His reward was the ability to conquer the next, and he told me that the enjoyment in the process was found in paying the same amount every month and knowing he was making progress. It was comforting to him to know he was on the right track and that it was happening automatically.

His approach to giving was also unorthodox during his five-year journey to freedom from debt. After tithing for his whole adult life, as he was growing deeper and deeper in debt, Ron felt the Lord told him that he could not play games anymore with God's money. Yes, he was tithing, but he was also quickly racking up major credit card debt. A light bulb went on one day for Ron when he realized that he was, in essence, putting his tithe on his credit card every month because he was not living within his means. Convinced he was being a poor steward by digging a deeper and deeper debt hole, Ron temporarily suspended his giving. Certainly, God's principles in the Bible concerning avoiding the dangers of debt are no less powerful and compelling than the principles dealing with giving. Just as you cannot say prayer is more important than forgiveness or that obedience is superior to grace, Ron was convinced the Lord was leading him to take a radical approach to attacking his debt because he was so convinced the Lord wanted him debt free. Some may not agree with this tactic, and I'm a proponent for giving while in debt-reduction mode— but Ron is a godly man who was under the Lord's leading. It's hard to argue with his results.

Immediately he felt he was being a much better steward of the money God was providing for him. After he had paid off his debts, he picked up right where he had left off with his giving. He wasted no time in giving 10 percent of his first check back to God, and he's been tithing to his church and giving generously to the work of God's kingdom ever since. He even automated his giving, and his monthly donations go directly from his bank account to the ministries he supports. Now, instead of making auto payments on a mountain of debt, he's making auto payments to God's work. What a terrific turnaround!

Ron followed the Lord's leading and closed his entrepreneurial business, and he landed a terrific job as a corporate lawyer. As someone who's known Ron for a long time, I can say it's been a treat for me to watch him flourish in his new position, turn his finances around, stay debt free, and get back on track with giving generously to the work of God's kingdom.

It all started with the desire to become automatically debt free. If you follow Ron's approach, you, too, can enjoy automatic discipline by using this effective and powerful payment system for becoming debt free.

CONCLUSION

May the God of all hope fill you with all joy and peace as you trust in him, so that you may overflow with hope by the power of the Holy Spirit *(Romans 15:13).*

As we see from Ron's story, getting out of debt requires a combination of gaining a new vision for a better way of handling the money God has given us, determination, submitting to the Lord, humility, self-control, and financial tactics that have been tested by time. The amount of money you make and the amount of your debt aren't really determining factors. You can do this with steady effort and God's help. You can employ the plan I've laid out here, and I've seen many people find financial peace and fitness in Christ through using these methods.

I pray that you'll begin to overflow with hope as you press on, with the Lord's help, to eliminate your debt. Set your sights on the Lord, set realistic goals for reducing your debt, and set up your automatic debt-reduction plan, which will lead you into financial freedom.

Joy and peace will come as you trust in Him, and no peace will appear apart from the power of the Holy Spirit. God be with you on your journey.

APPENDIX

Abundant Living: The Freedom Principle

Sample Debt Reduction Plan

DEBT	BALANCE DUE	INTEREST RATE	MINIMUM PAYMENT	EXTRA PAYMENT	TOTAL PAYMENT
1. Visa	$225	16%	$10	$50	$60
2. Dept. Store	$3,015	24%	$60	$0	$60
3. Furniture Store	$2,200	22%	$45	$0	$45
4. Bank Card	$1,300	15%	$30	$0	$30
5. Gas Card	$235	10%	$10	$0	$10
Total Debt:	**$6,975**	**Total Monthly Payment:**			**$205**

Strategy

1. The smallest debt was listed first on purpose for motivational purposes (Plan Point #3).

2. You will pay $205 a month (or more if available) on debts until you are out of debt. If more funds become available, add them to the debt at the top of the list.

3. Once Visa is paid in full, add the $60 payment to the department store payment, and begin paying $120 each month until it is paid off. Continue paying minimum payments on other debts.

4. Once the department store is paid off, add the $120 payment to the furniture store payment, and begin paying $185 a month until it is paid off. Follow this pattern until all debts are paid off. Continue paying minimum payments on other debts.

Abundant Living: The Freedom Principle

Your Personal Debt Reduction Plan

DEBT	BALANCE DUE	INTEREST RATE	MINIMUM PAYMENT	EXTRA PAYMENT	TOTAL PAYMENT
1.					
2.					
3.					
4.					
5.					
6.					
7.					
8.					
9.					
10.					
Total Debt:		**Total Monthly Payment:**			

Notes:

NOTES

Introduction

1. "Americans Donate Billions to Charity, but Giving to Churches Has Declined," Barna Research Group, April 25, 2005, <www.barna.org>.

Chapter 3

1. <http://app1.sba.gov/faqs/faqindex.cfm?areaID=24>.

2. By the numbers section, John Macintyre, *Spirit Magazine*, October 2005.

3. <http://www.finaid.org/loans/>.

4. Associated Press quoting *Consumer Reports*, Feb. 28, 2007.

5. <http://www.hotpayday.com/fee.html>.

Chapter 5

1. <http://www.40debts.org/counseling/DebtManagement/FAQ.asp>.